Text by Paola Misesti
Illustrations by Federica Fusi

TRACE WITH ME

MY FIRST PRE-WRITING ACTIVITY BOOK

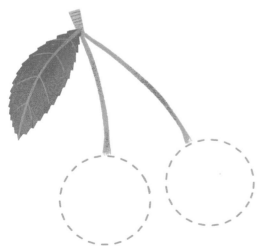

STERLING CHILDREN'S BOOKS
New York

INTRODUCTION TO PRE-WRITING

Pre-writing activities prepare young children to learn how to write.

The act of writing requires many skills. Writing involves translating sounds into symbols, and making very precise movements to reproduce those symbols on the page. At the same time, the writer must connect what the hand is doing with the meaning of the written word.

We can think of writing as "words in movement." The movement is quite complex, and it requires training. Through repetition and coordination, pre-writing activities train the hand to make movements that become increasingly precise and controlled. They're exercises that develop the skills necessary for proper writing.

Pre-writing is not the same as free drawing, where children can freely express their creativity. It serves a different purpose: improving their visual perception and manual dexterity, along with working on coordination and precision.

This book presents many different activities in the form of a game, so that children can practice pre-writing skills while having fun. By following the adventures of Prose, a little alien, children will engage in varied and stimulating tasks on every page.

WHAT TYPE OF ACTIVITIES ARE IN THIS BOOK?

-Exercises designed to train and refine coordination and precision by asking children to draw along a dotted line

-Activities that aim at improving motor planning (the process of visualizing a task, planning the steps required, and executing the correct movements to complete it), such as coloring inside the borders of a drawing

-Exercises to develop fine motor skills using scissors or stickers

-Attention and logic games, such as pairing images and working through mazes

To begin, you can encourage children to use the small space shuttle included with the stickers at the end of the book to complete some of the activities without a pencil. Children can build the shuttle by following the instructions included in this book. After the shuttle has been put together, they will be able to use it to follow dotted lines, slowly allowing them to get used to the hand movements.

It is important for children to feel independent when doing the activities. By experiencing the activities as a game, without pressure or fear of making mistakes, children will feel more encouraged to complete each one.

However, adults still have the important task of telling the story of the little alien, reading the instructions, explaining the exercises, and suggesting suitable materials for each activity, such as: crayons, stickers, pencils, or scissors.

READY?
LET'S START!

ON A PLANET FAR, FAR AWAY...

Hello, my name is **PROSE**. I'm not a human, like you. I come from a remote planet. As you can see, I have four arms, four eyes, and a big nose. My **ANTENNAE** are special because they show my emotions.

JOIN THE DOTTED LINE THAT CONNECTS MY ANTENNAE, AND USE THE STICKERS TO HELP ME COMPLETE MY OUTFIT!

THE SPACE SHUTTLE FACTORY

I've heard a lot about your planet: **EARTH**. I would like to visit it, but it is far away and I need a special shuttle to reach it.

USE THE STICKERS IN THE BACK OF THE BOOK TO PUT MY SHUTTLE TOGETHER. THE GUIDE BELOW WILL HELP YOU PUT THE PIECES IN THE RIGHT ORDER.

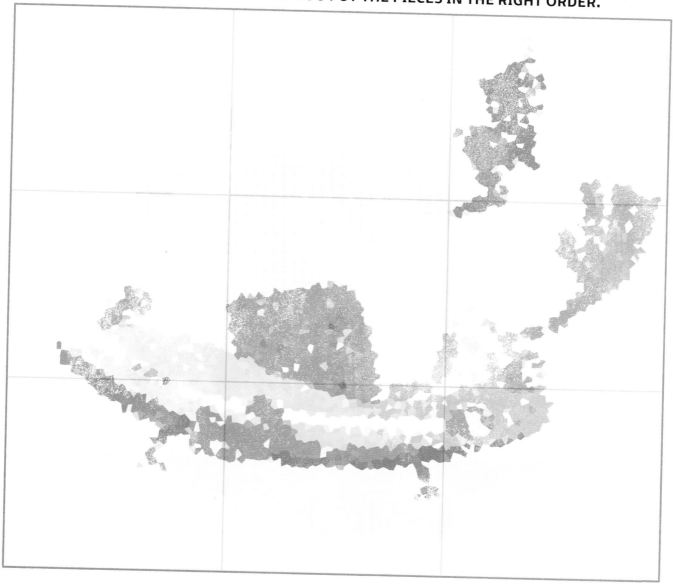

A mini version of my shuttle is included with the stickers at the back of this book. You can use it to help me find my way around before you start using a pencil. **PUT THE STICKER ON A PIECE OF CARDBOARD AND CUT ALONG ITS BORDERS, AND YOU WILL BE READY TO START YOUR JOURNEY WITH ME!**

THE LONG JOURNEY BEGINS...

Space is truly enormous. There are so many beautiful planets!
I need to be careful to **AVOID CRASHING INTO THEM**.

It's not easy,
but I can do it with your help.

CONNECT THE DOTTED LINES AROUND THE PLANETS TO HELP ME AVOID THEM.

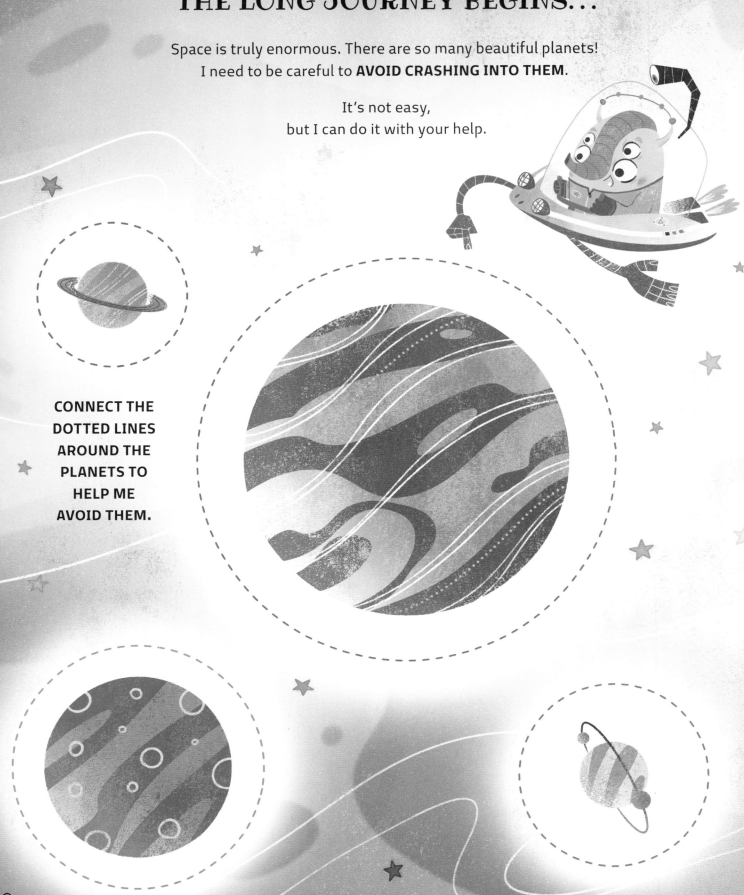

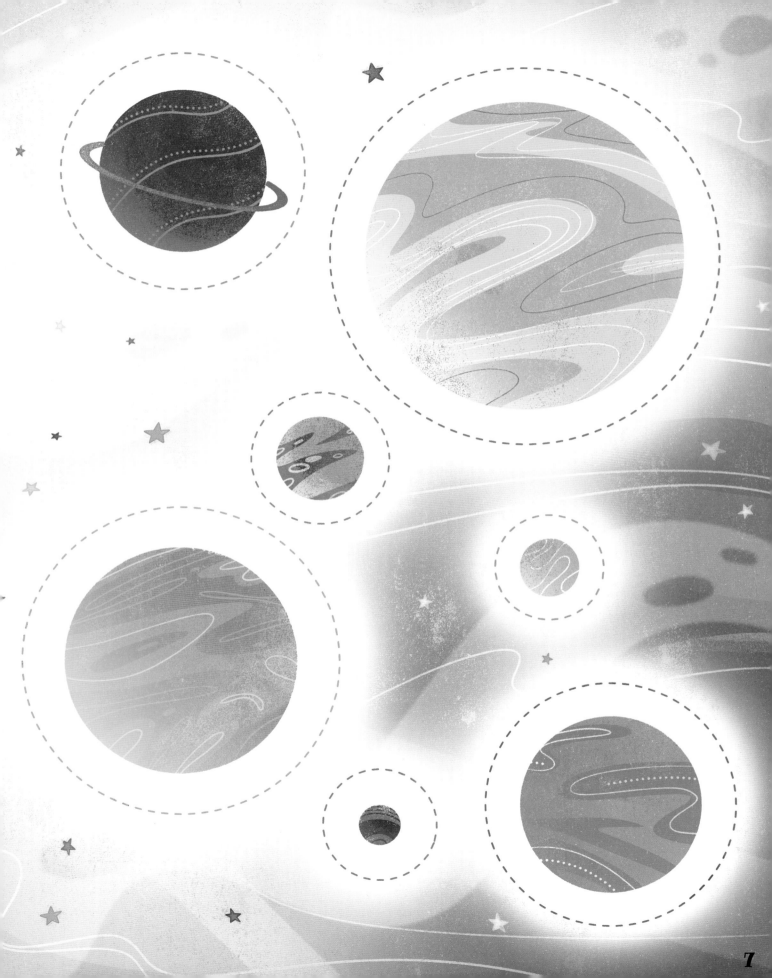

STROLLING THROUGH SPACE

I'm almost there! Help me finish my journey to Earth.

**FIND A ROUTE THAT TAKES ME TO YOU,
AVOIDING PLANETS AND STARS.**

EARTH

A STORM IS COMING!

Something strange is happening. What's all that water coming down from the sky? You call it **RAIN**. It seems exciting, but also a bit dangerous.

DRAW THE RAIN BY CONNECTING THE DOTTED LINES. MAKE SURE THE RAIN DOESN'T HIT MY SHUTTLE.

THE WIND DANCE

What's happening? A strong **WIND** is coming through,
blowing my spaceship off course. If I could see the gusts
of wind, I could avoid them. Can you help me?

**DRAW THE GUSTS BY CONNECTING
THE DOTTED LINES.**

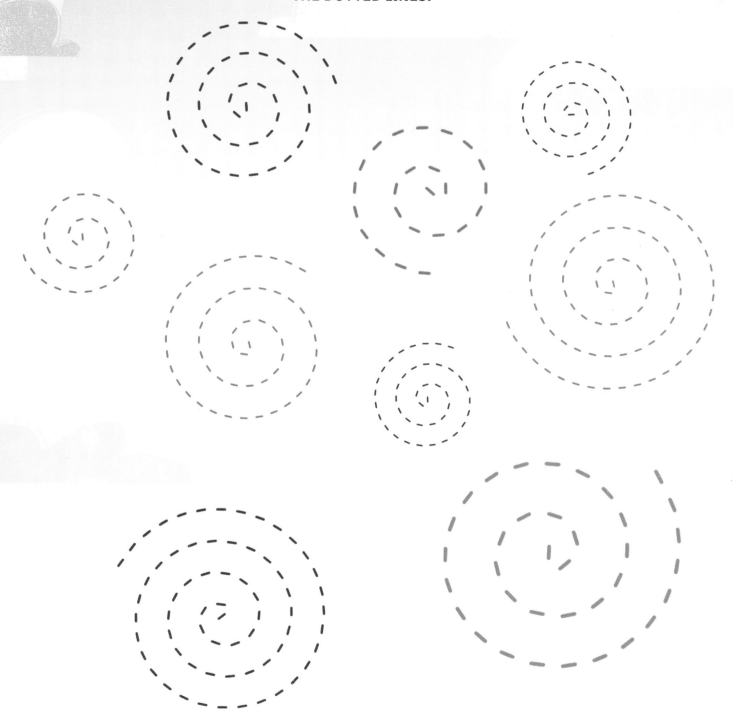

DISCOVERING COLORS

Wow, a **RAINBOW!** It is made up of a lot of wonderful colors, but I can't see them very well.

CONNECT EACH DOTTED LINE. THEN COLOR IN BETWEEN THEM TO FINISH THE RAINBOW.

A HAPPY WELCOME

WHO'S TWEETING NOW? Oh, here are some little birds coming to say hello to me!
It's too sunny, though, and I can't see them very well.

**LINK EACH BIRD TO ITS SHADOW, SO THAT
I CAN RECOGNIZE WHICH BIRD IS WHICH.**

THE ZIGZAGGING
SHUTTLE

MOUNTAINS are beautiful, but they
are also very sharp. I need to avoid them.
Can you help me?

**CONNECT THE DOTTED LINES
TO HELP MY SHUTTLE
AVOID THE PEAKS.**

A THUNDEROUS RIVER

If I want to reach the ocean,
I need to follow the river.

**CAN YOU HELP ME FIND
THE RIGHT PATH?**

A TRULY SPECIAL ENCOUNTER

I like the ocean a lot. It is home to many nice creatures, like this cute and colorful **OCTOPUS**.

COMPLETE IT BY USING THE STICKERS AT THE BACK OF THE BOOK AND CONNECTING THE DOTTED LINE.

FISH IN SHAPE

These funny fish all have strange, unique shapes!

**DRAW ALONG THE DOTTED LINES
TO DISCOVER THEIR SHAPES
WITH ME.**

A FRIENDLY ROUTE

The sea is also full of **SHARKS** with big teeth that seem a little scary.
The little fish promised to show me a safe route. Can you help me, too?

**FOLLOW THE FISH, CONNECTING THE LINES ON
THE ROUTE THEY ARE SHOWING YOU.**

A MAP AT THE BOTTOM OF THE SEA

The ocean is big, and full of animals and rip currents. I was afraid I would get lost.
Luckily, the dolphins offered to guide me to shore!

**CAN YOU HELP ME FOLLOW
THE DOLPHINS' ROUTE? TRACE
IT WITH THE MINI-SHUTTLE
OR A PENCIL.**

A BEAUTIFUL FIELD

This is a wonderful field, and it smells lovely!
There are so many pretty and unique **FLOWERS**!

CONNECT THE DOTTED LINES TO COMPLETE THEM.

A FEAST FOR THE BEES

There are **BEES** buzzing above the **FLOWERS**. It seems like they are having fun! Look at how they all fly playfully!

**CONNECT THE DOTS TO FOLLOW THE BEES' PATHS.
THEN ADD FLOWER STICKERS
TO COMPLETE THE SCENE BELOW.**

THE HOUSE OF THE SNAILS

The snails are so pretty with their little houses on their backs.

DRAW THE SNAIL SHELLS BY CONNECTING THE DOTTED LINES.

LEAPING RABBITS

The rabbits can jump really high!

CONNECT THE DOTTED PATH LINES SO I CAN AVOID THE RABBITS.

LOST IN THE WOODS

I think I am lost. Can you find the path through all these trees
that will lead me to the barn?

**MARK THE PATH WITH A PENCIL, AND USE
STICKERS TO NOTE ANY INTERESTING PLANTS
OR ANIMALS YOU SEE ON THE WAY.**

HIDING ON THE FARM

I like the animals on this farm. They want to play hide-and-seek with me.
Can you help me find them?

**LOOK FOR THESE ANIMALS ON THE FARM.
CIRCLE EACH ANIMAL WHEN YOU FIND IT.**

A BELLY FULL OF FRUIT

After playing, I feel hungry. I like fruit, but I don't know what it looks like here on your planet. Can you show me where the fruit is below?

DRAW ALONG THE DOTTED LINES AND COLOR IN THE FRUIT. AVOID ANYTHING ELSE SO THAT I DON'T EAT IT BY MISTAKE!

CITY-BOUND

I would like to find out what a city looks like,
but the route is full of obstacles.

**CAN YOU BE MY NAVIGATOR
AND DRAW MY ROUTE?**

UP AND DOWN
ABOVE THE CITY

I wasn't expecting all these buildings.
Some of them are so tall!
Flying up and down is a lot of fun.

**TRY TO FOLLOW
THE DOTTED LINE,
AVOIDING HOUSES
AND SKYSCRAPERS.**

TRAIN JAM

There are so many trains in this big city!
Each one is going to a different station, but the tracks are broken
and the trains have all stopped. I would like to help them.

CAN YOU HELP ME FIX THE TRACKS? CONNECT THE DOTTED LINES SO THAT THE TRAINS CAN CONTINUE THEIR JOURNEY.

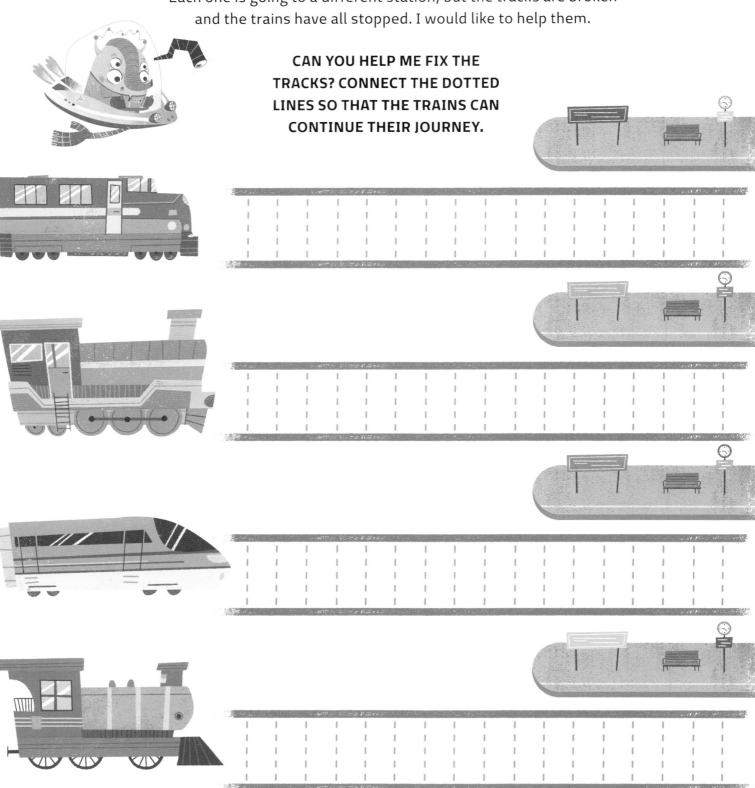

DRIVING ADVENTURES

The city is packed with cars, and it is very interesting
to see how they move. Try to drive!

**BUILD THE DIE THAT YOU FIND AT THE END
OF THE BOOK, THROW IT,
AND DRAW THE LINE THAT
THE DIE SHOWS INSIDE ONE
OF THE ARROWS BELOW.**

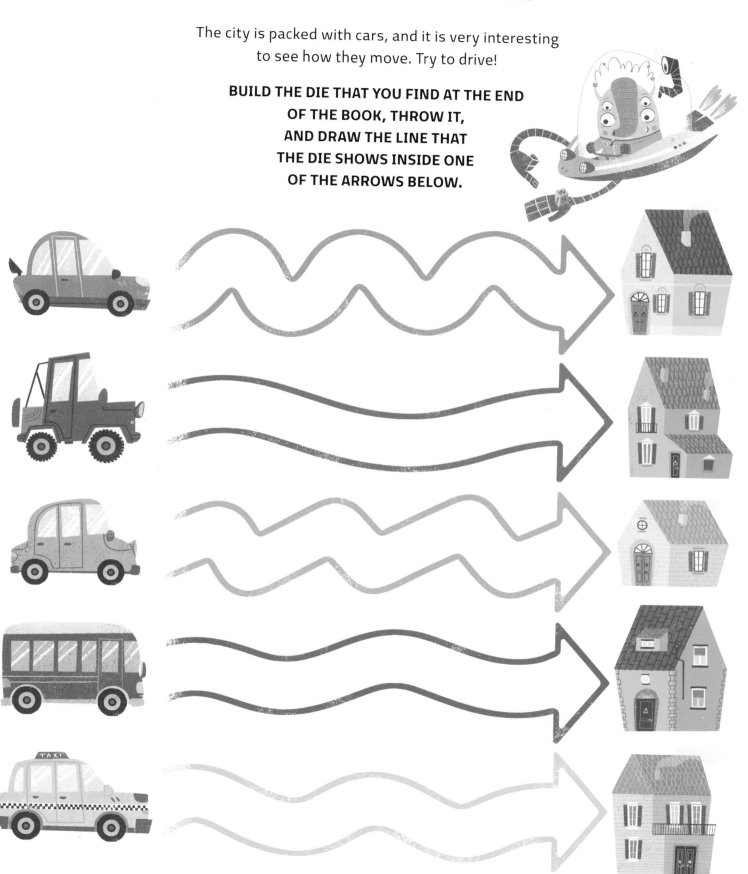

TIME TO GO BACK

It's time for me to go back home. All my friends are waiting for me.
They are excited to hear about my adventure on planet Earth with you.

**BUT GOING BACK HOME CAN BE DIFFICULT.
CAN YOU SHOW ME THE ROUTE BY CONNECTING
THE LINE CREATED BY THE STARS?**

PAOLA MISESTI

Born in Como in 1970, she has lived in Zurich with her family since 2011. She is a pedagogist and has written and co-written many articles on pedagogy. She also teaches Italian. For many years, she has trained educators, teachers, and parents, and has created workshops and educational projects for primary schools. For the past ten years, she has been sharing her experiences and materials online, through her website www.homemademamma.com.

FEDERICA FUSI

Born in Massa Marittima, Tuscany, and forever passionate about drawing, she received a diploma from the School of Arts in Grosseto, then obtained a degree in art from the Academy of Fine Arts in Florence. She specializes in visual arts and new expressive languages in painting. She also studied illustration at the Nemo Academy of Digital Art in Florence, attending the course on entertainment design. She currently lives in Florence, where she teaches and works as an illustrator.

STERLING CHILDREN'S BOOKS
New York

An Imprint of Sterling Publishing Co., Inc.
1166 Avenue of the Americas
New York, NY 10036

ISBN 973-1-4549-4382-2

For information about custom editions, special sales, and premium and corporate purchases, please contact Sterling Special Sales at 800-805-5489 or specialsales@sterlingpublishing.com.

Manufactured in China

Lot #:
2 4 6 8 10 9 7 5 3 1
07/21

sterlingpublishing.com

Design by Valentina Figus
Illustrated by Federica Fusi - Translation by Inga Sempel

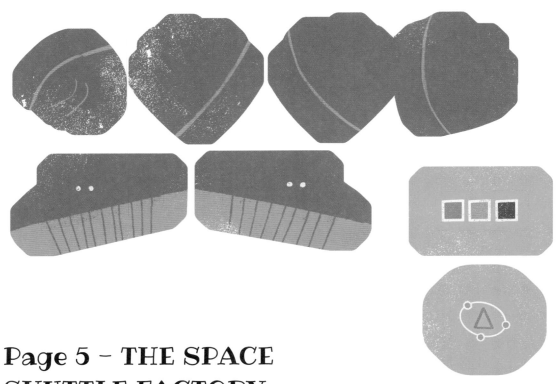

Page 5 – THE SPACE SHUTTLE FACTORY

THE SPACE
SHUTTLE FACTORY

Page 18 – A TRULY SPECIAL ENCOUNTER

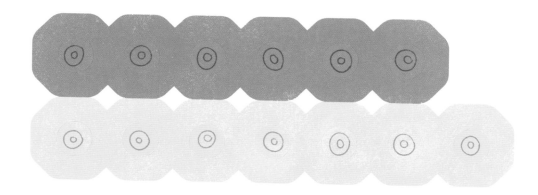

Pages 24-25 - A FEAST FOR THE BEES

Pages 28-29 - LOST IN THE WOODS

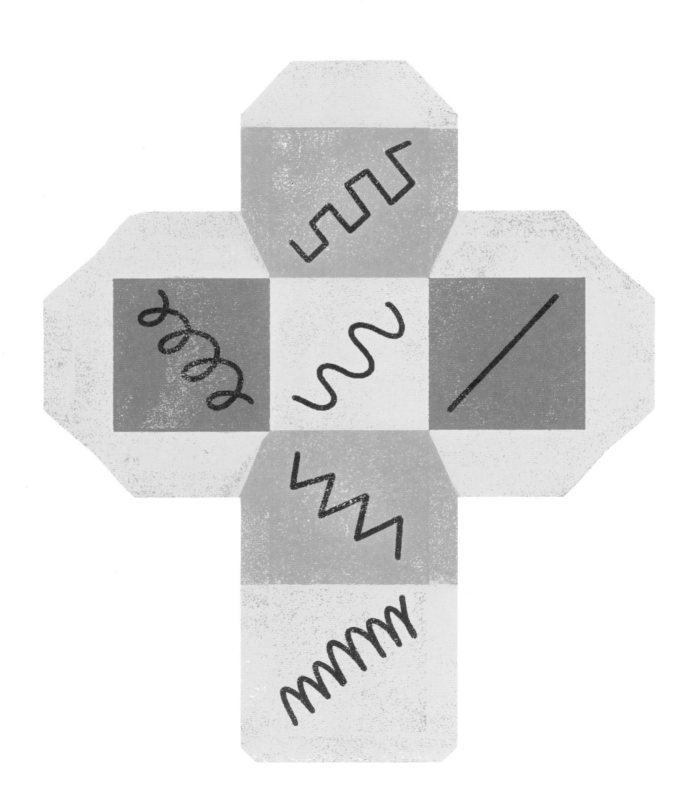

USE THESE STICKERS TO PERSONALIZE YOUR DRAWINGS